HEAD, SHOULDERS, KNEES AND TOES

IN SPANISH

with English Translations

First Edition

Authored by
Gerard Aflague

Spanish translations by
East-West Concepts
www.eastwestconcepts.com

Edited by
Mary Aflague

Published by the
GERÅRD AFLÅGUE COLLECTION
Copyright 2017

Head, Shoulders, Knees and Toes teaches kids their body parts in Spanish with English translations.

This book is dedicated to

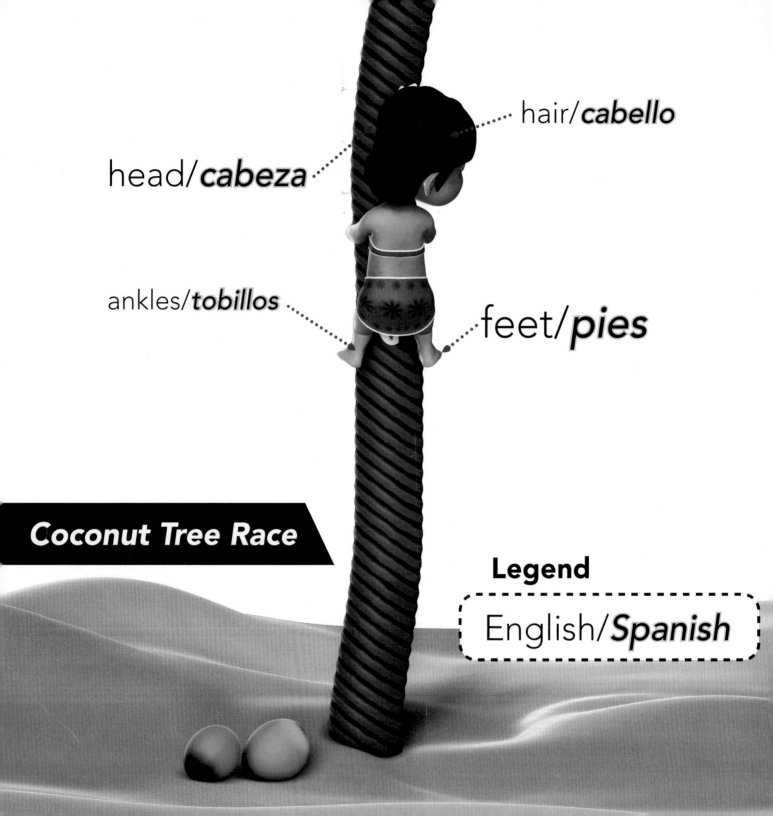

hair/*cabello*

head/*cabeza*

ankles/*tobillos*

feet/*pies*

Coconut Tree Race

Legend

English/*Spanish*

How do you say **hair**?
[in Spanish]

Touch your *cabeza*?

How do you say **ankles**?
[in Spanish]

Wiggle your *pies*?

Point to your *codo*?

How do you say **nose**?
[in Spanish]

What are *dedos de los pies*?

How do you say **back**?
[in Spanish]

eyelashes / *pestañas*

eyes/*ojos*

pupil/*pupila*

ear lobe/ *lóbulo de oreja*

mouth/*boca*

thigh/*muslo*

Diversión en el océano azul

Adam's apple [males]/
manzana de Adán

chin/**barbilla**

lips/**labios**

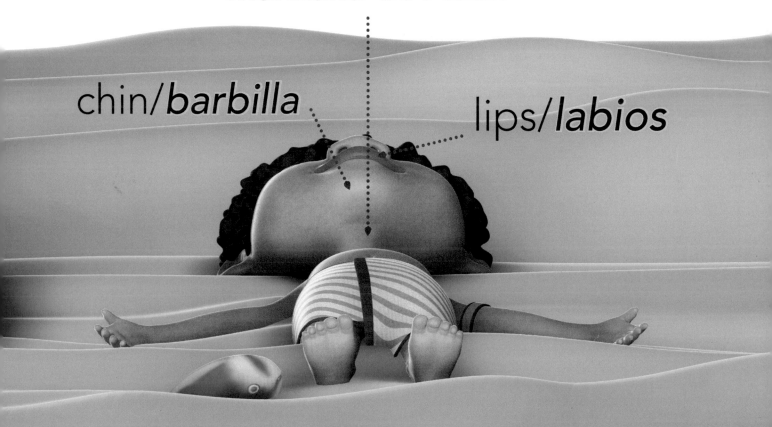

How do you say **eyelashes**?
[in Spanish]

Point to your *ojos*?

How do you say **pupil**?
[in Spanish]

Where is your *boca*?

How do you say **lips**?
[in Spanish]

Pull your *lóbulo de oreja*?

How do you say **thigh**?
[in Spanish]

Touch your *barbilla*?

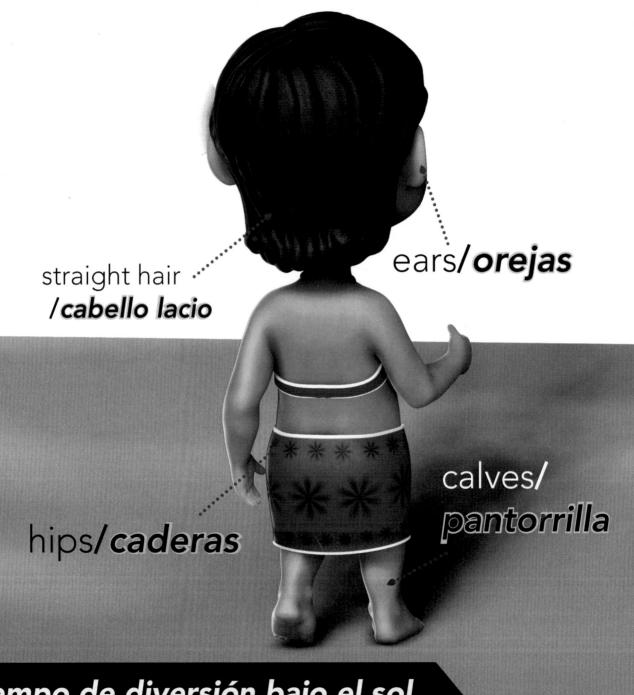

straight hair
/**cabello lacio**

ears/**orejas**

hips/**caderas**

calves/
pantorrilla

Tiempo de diversión bajo el sol

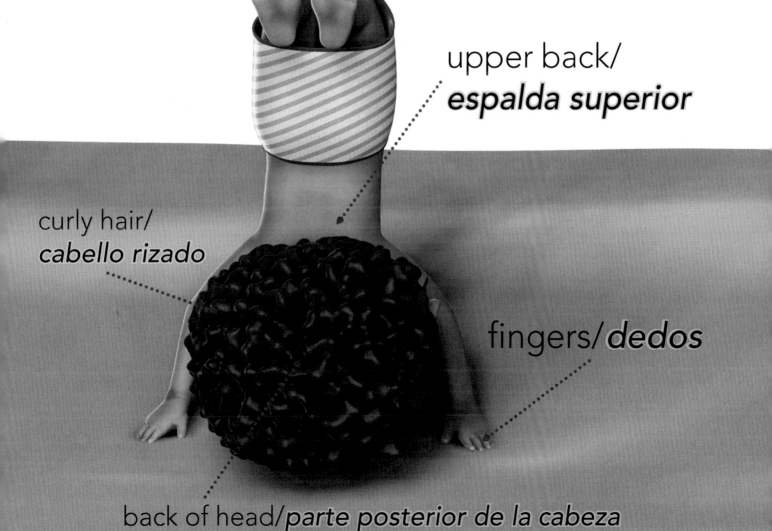

upper back/
espalda superior

curly hair/
cabello rizado

fingers/*dedos*

back of head/*parte posterior de la cabeza*

How do you say **ears**?
[in Spanish]

Place your hands on your *caderas*?

How do you say **calves**?
[in Spanish]

What is *cabello lacio*?

What is **cabello rizado**?

How do you say **upper back**?
[in Spanish]

Wiggle your **dedos**?

How do you say **back of head**?

[in Spanish]

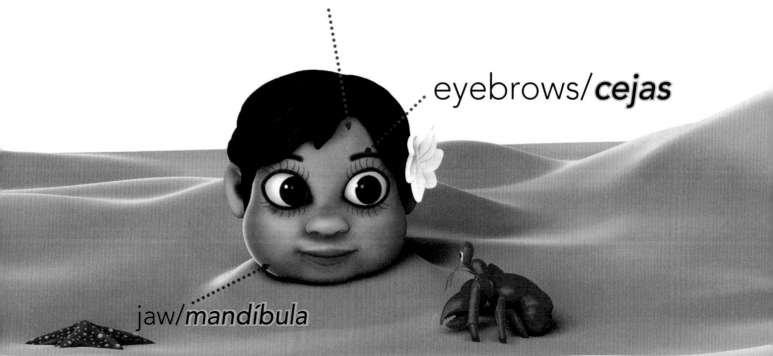

forehead/***frente***

eyebrows/***cejas***

jaw/***mandíbula***

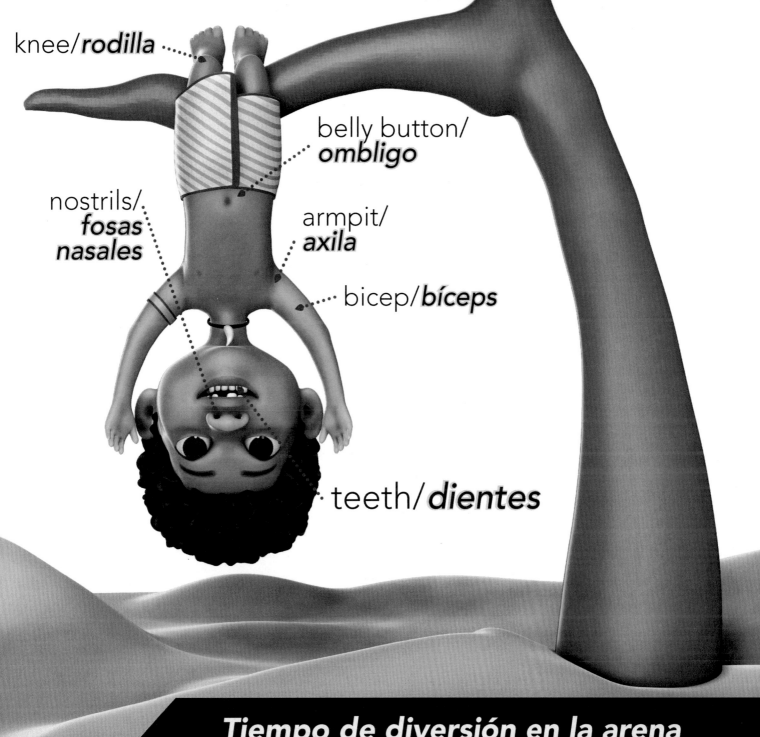

knee/**rodilla**

belly button/**ombligo**

nostrils/**fosas nasales**

armpit/**axila**

bicep/**bíceps**

teeth/**dientes**

Tiempo de diversión en la arena

How do you say **eyebrows**?

[in Spanish]

Touch your *mandíbula*?

How do you say **forehead**?

[in Spanish]

Find your *rodilla*?

How do you say **teeth**?

[in Spanish]

Touch your *ombligo*?

How do you say **nostrils**?

[in Spanish]

Find your *axila*?

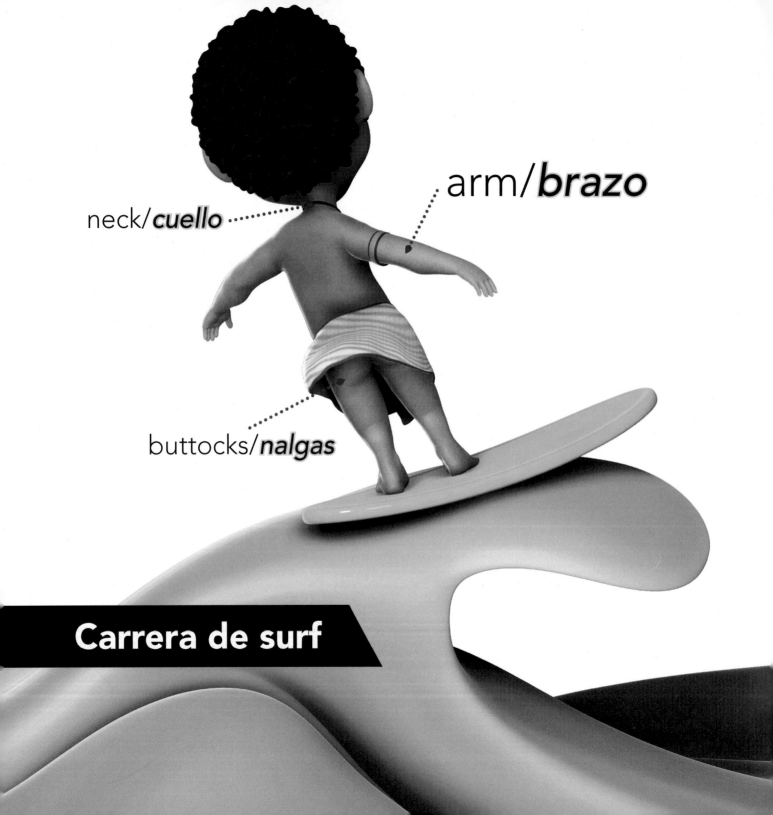

neck/*cuello*

arm/*brazo*

buttocks/*nalgas*

Carrera de surf

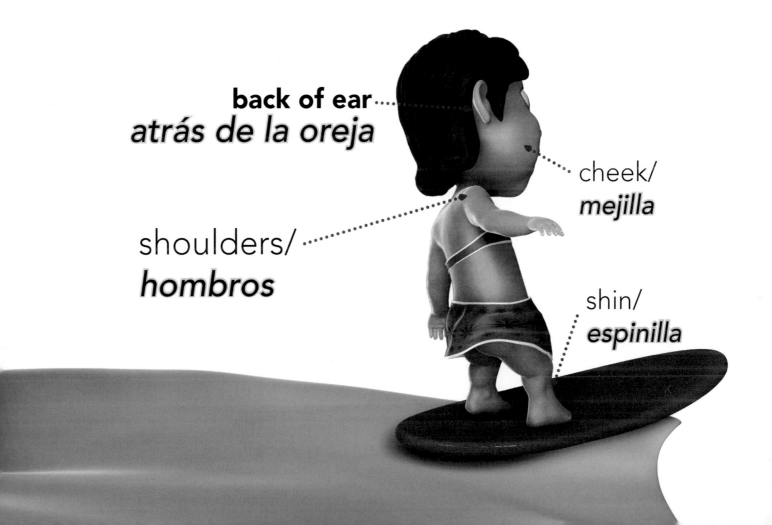

back of ear
atrás de la oreja

cheek/
mejilla

shoulders/
hombros

shin/
espinilla

Point to your *cuello*?

How do you say **arm**?
[in Spanish]

Find your *nalgas*?

How do you say **shoulders**?
[in Spanish]

Touch your *mejilla*?

How do you say **shin**?
[in Spanish]

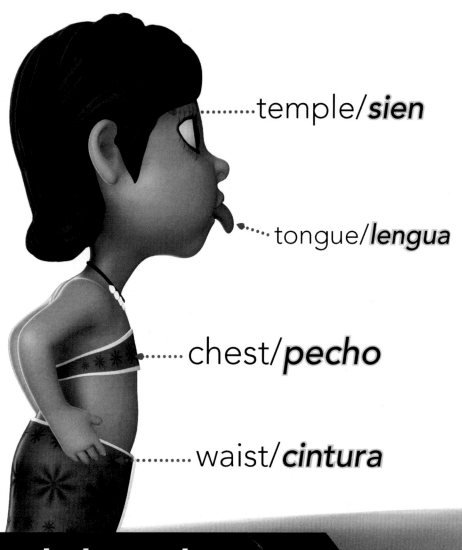

temple/*sien*

tongue/*lengua*

chest/*pecho*

waist/*cintura*

Tiempo de hacer bromas

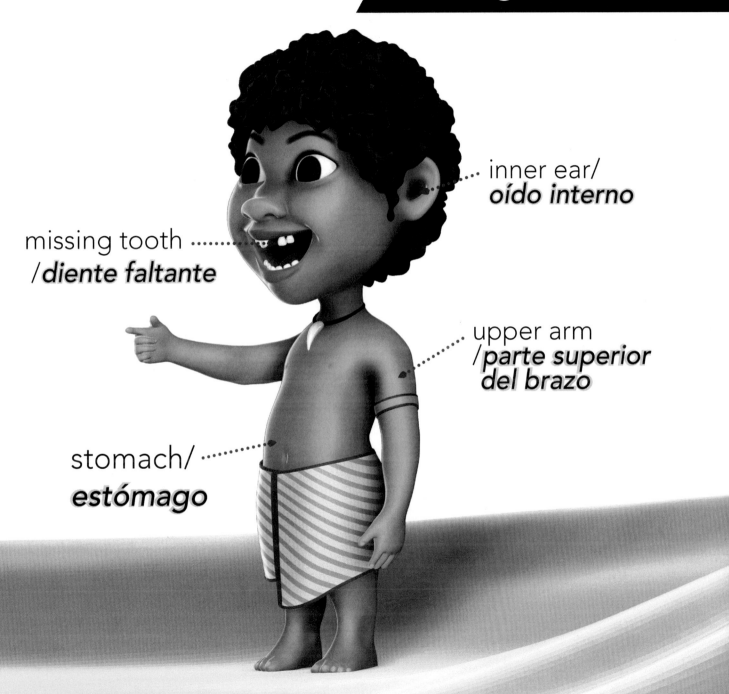

inner ear/
oído interno

missing tooth
/*diente faltante*

upper arm
/*parte superior
del brazo*

stomach/
estómago

How do you say **tongue**?
[in Spanish]

Where is your *sien*?

How do you say **chest**?
[in Spanish]

Put your hands on your *cintura*?

Touch your *parte superior del brazo*?

How do you say **inner ear**?
[in Spanish]

Touch your *estómago*?

How do you say **missing tooth**?
[in Spanish]

Pescado sorpresa

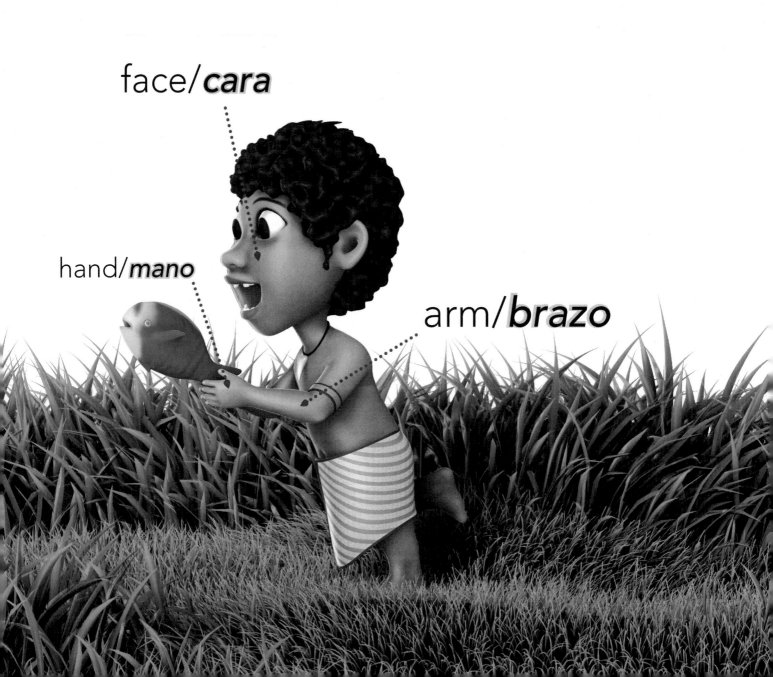

face/*cara*

hand/*mano*

arm/*brazo*

Fishy Surprise

skin/*piel*

legs/
piernas

upper body/
parte superior del cuerpo

How do you say **arm**?
[in Spanish]

Raise your *mano*?

How do you say **face**?
[in Spanish]

Touch your *piel*?

How do you say **upper body**?
[in Spanish]

Where are your *piernas*?

It's time to test your knowledge!

Test Section

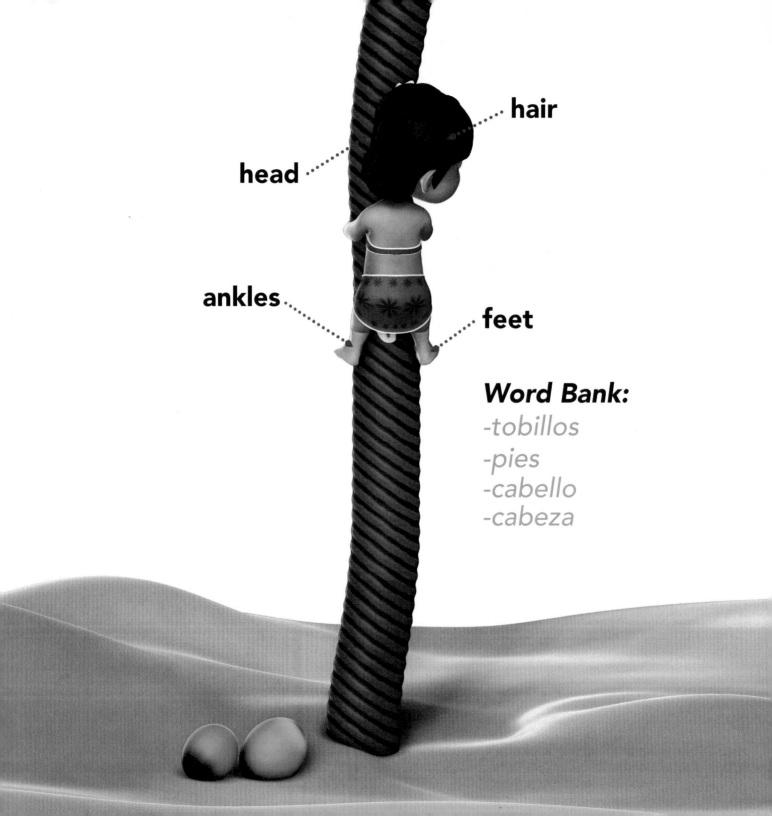

hair

head

ankles

feet

Word Bank:
-tobillos
-pies
-cabello
-cabeza

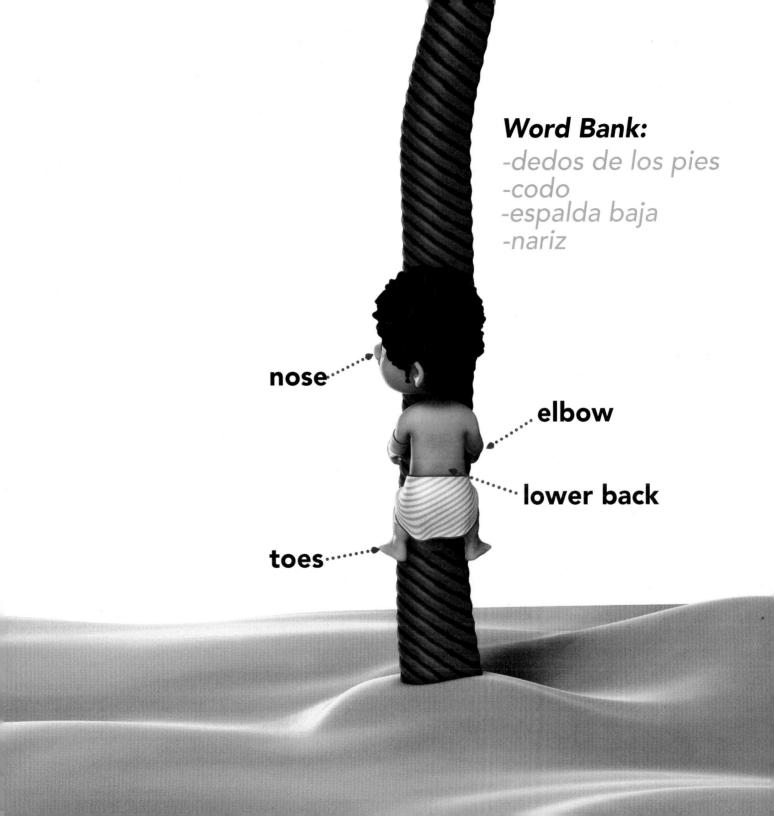

Word Bank:
-dedos de los pies
-codo
-espalda baja
-nariz

nose

elbow

lower back

toes

eyelashes

eyes

pupil

mouth

Word Bank:
-muslo
-lóbulo de oreja
-boca
-ojos
-pestañas
-pupila

ear lobe

thigh

Word Bank:

- labios
- manzana de Adán
- barbilla

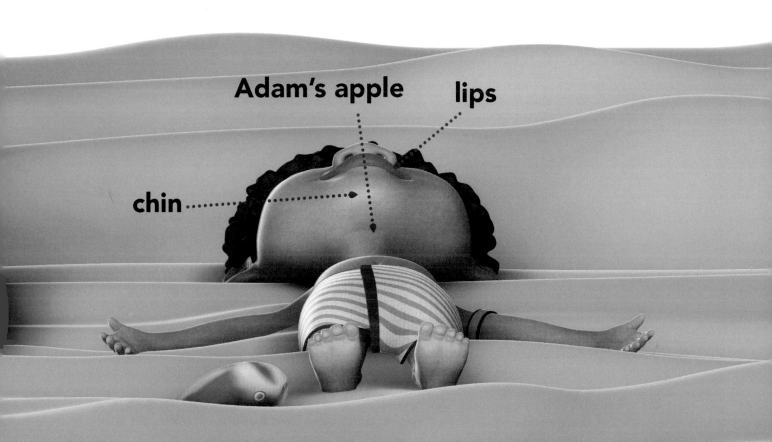

Adam's apple · · · · · · · · · · lips

chin · · · · · · · · · · · · · · · · · ·

Word Bank:
-caderas
-orejas
-cabello lacio
-pantorrilla

straight hair ....

ears

hips ....

calves

upper back

curly hair

fingers

back of head

Word Bank:
-mandíbula
-cejas
-frente

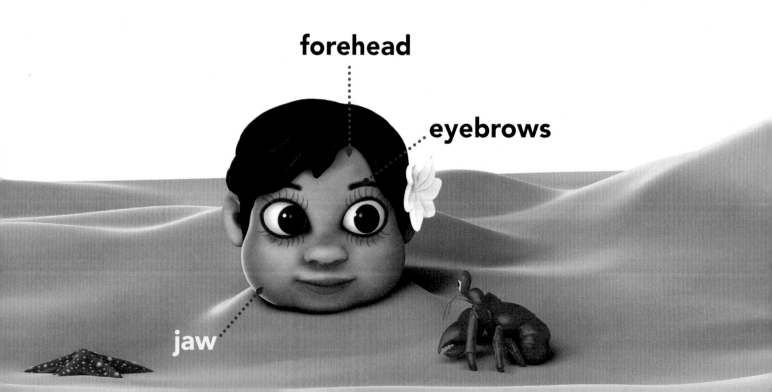

forehead

eyebrows

jaw

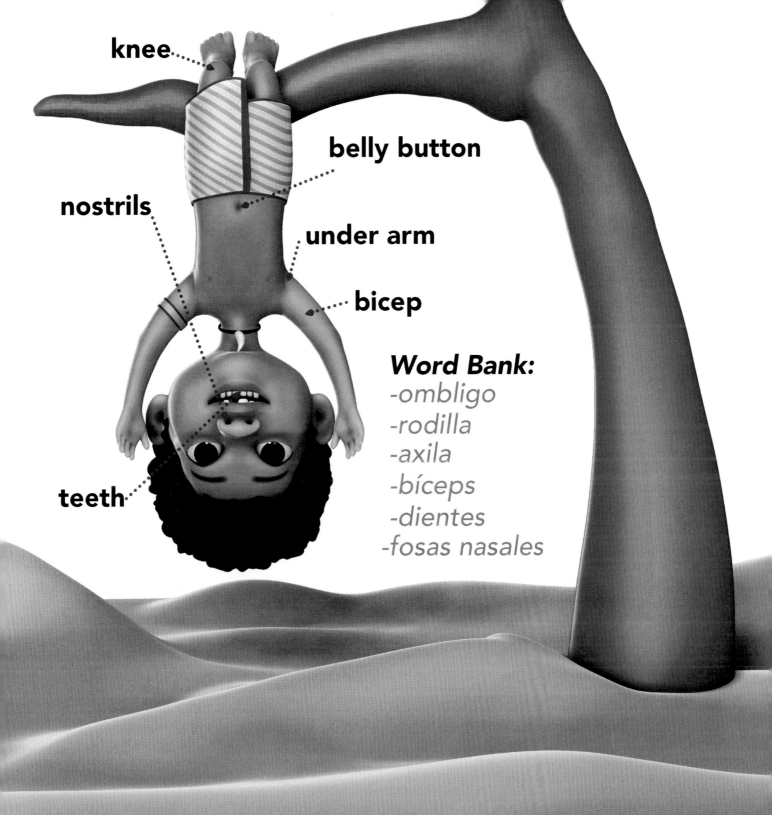

knee

belly button

nostrils

under arm

bicep

teeth

Word Bank:
-ombligo
-rodilla
-axila
-bíceps
-dientes
-fosas nasales

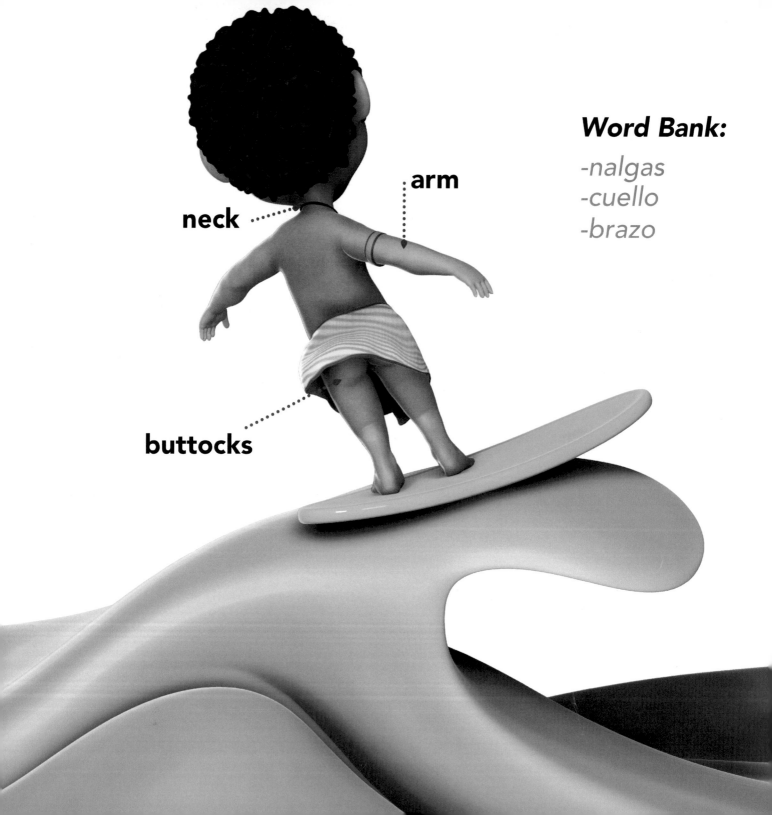

neck

arm

buttocks

Word Bank:
-nalgas
-cuello
-brazo

Word Bank:

-atrás de la oreja
-hombros
-mejilla
-espinilla

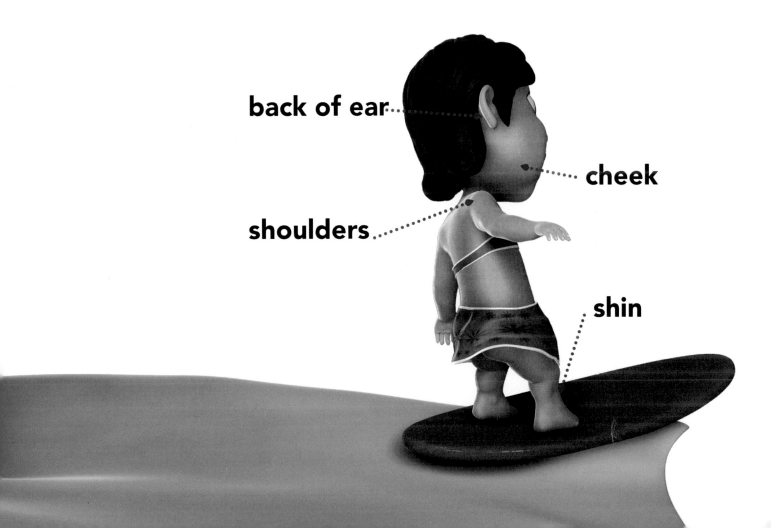

back of ear

cheek

shoulders

shin

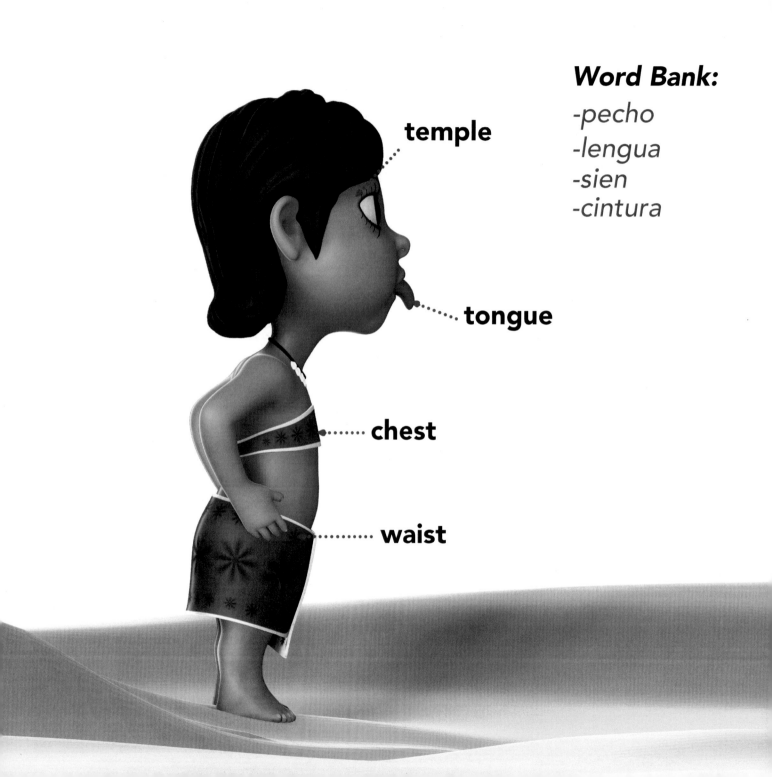

temple

tongue

chest

waist

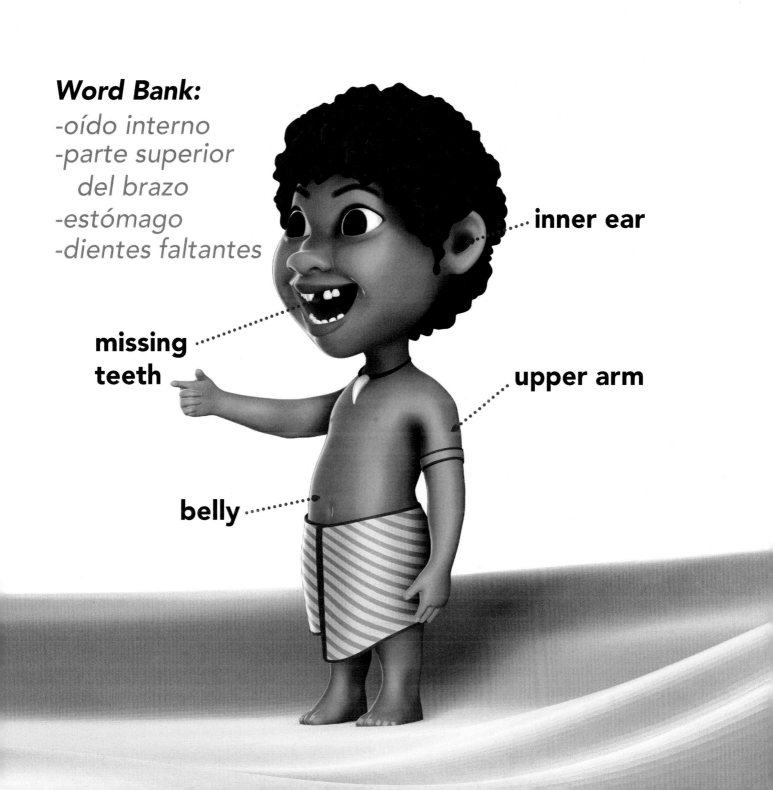

Word Bank:
- oído interno
- parte superior del brazo
- estómago
- dientes faltantes

inner ear

missing teeth

upper arm

belly

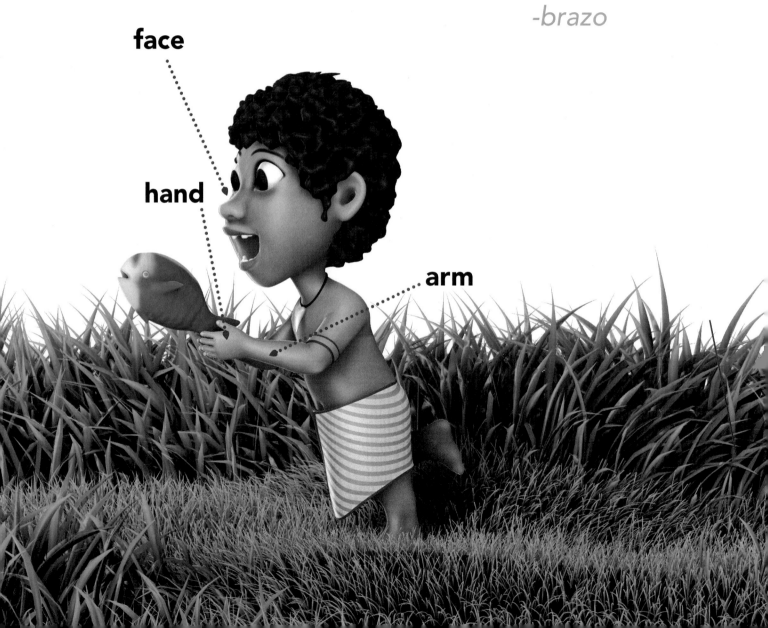

face

hand

arm

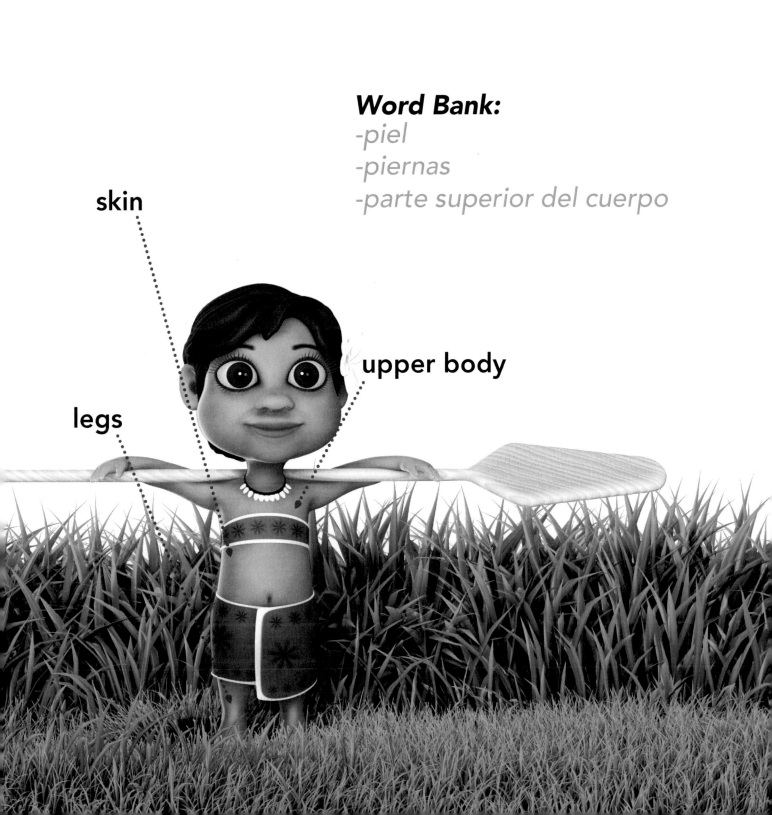

Word Bank:
-piel
-piernas
-parte superior del cuerpo

skin

upper body

legs

See other interesting titles from the Gerard Aflague Collection

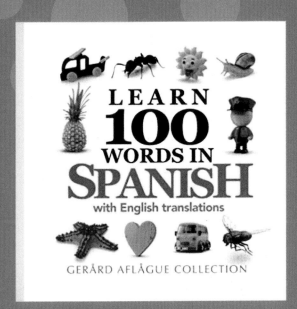

Teach children 100 words in Spanish.

In no time, they will be able to a variety of things in Spanish.

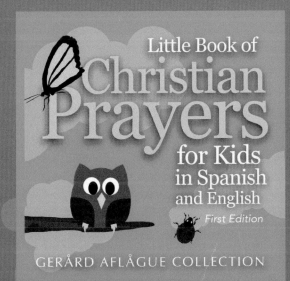

Teach children how to pray in Spanish.

With five basic prayers in this book.

About the Author

Mary Aflague was born and raised on the beautiful island of Guam. Now residing in Colorado, she still manages to enjoy the outdoors and sunshine. She is a long time educator and continues to instill in both her children and students, the joy and power of being life-long readers and learners. Her interests include reading, yoga, Zentangle Art, traveling, and Pacific Island dance.

About the Designer

Gerard Aflague is a long-time Guam native who resides in Highlands Ranch, Colorado. Gerard enjoys illustrating and publishing cultural books that inspire, educate, and entertain. He also helps others publish their books under his collection. In addition to publishing, he also writes, designs products, and manages his own online retail store. When he is not dreaming up new products for his collection, he spends time with family traveling, trying exotic food, or reading a good book.